Sleepwalking Among the Camels

SLEEPWALKING AMONG THE CAMELS

NEW AND SELECTED POEMS

TOM KONYVES

EDITED BY KEN NORRIS

© 1995, Tom Konyves

All rights reserved. No part of this book may be reproduced, stored in a retrieval system or transmitted in any form or by any means without written permission from The Muses' Company, an imprint of J. Gordon Shillingford Publishing Inc., except for brief excerpts used in critical reviews

Cover design by Terry Gallagher/Doowah Design
Cover art © Francis Picabia/Kinemage, Montreal, 1995
Author photo by Sai Goh

Published with the assistance of The Canada Council

Printed and bound in Canada by Hignell Printing

Canadian Cataloguing in Publication Data

Konyves, Tom, 1947-
    Sleepwalking among the camels: new & selected poetry

ISBN 0-919754-58-9

    I. Title.

PS8571.O724S54 1995   C811'.54   C95-900752-0
PR9199.3.K636S54 1995

The Muses' Company
P.O. Box 214, Ste. Anne de Bellevue, Québec, Canada H9X 3R9

For *Marlene, Michael, Alexander, Gabriel, Hannah, Ken* and *Martin*

Table of Contents

Introduction 9

No Parking (1978)

On a Line by Keats 25
Opus 7 26
Wordlessly 27
To Dawn 28
Heaven 31
Rebekah 32
Winter Allegory 33
Concrete Magnified 34
I'll Take the Tab 35
The Golden Calf in Technicolor 36
Phoenix 37
Art 38
Spring 39
Leonard Found Poem 40
Do Not Be Afraid of Death by Drowning 41
On the Suicidal Death of Pierre Paradis 42
Were Men, It Is 43
Peacock 45
Words Can Never Say 46
No Parking 47

Poetry in Performance (1982)

Sympathies of War 53
Yellow Light Blues 57
See/Saw 61
Ubu's Blues 73

Ex Perimeter (1988)

Montreal Lane Vision 85
The Leaves in November 86
The Last Days 87
The Funeral 88
At the Pik-Nik 89
To L.D. 90
Hallowe'en 91
Christmas Eve 1980 92
To New York 93
Ten Poems Around the Block 95
Approaching Guerrillas 100
My Dear Mary 101
Vancouver Rag 102
English Bay Vision 103
Birds at Qualicum 104
On the Birth of Alexander 105
Four Quarts 106
A Vision of Bureaucracy, After Kafka 108
The Tree of Singing Birds 109

Into This Space

Thus Spoke Tzarathustra 113
Blues at the Rising Sun 115
From the Rainbucket to the Lawnmower 118
For Leonard 119
Motions 120
Flamenco 122
Hopscotch 123
Percussion 124
Around the Point 125
Lost and Found 128
Into This Space 129

Introduction

"Words Can Never Say": The Poetry of Tom Konyves

Tom Konyves' poetry is fundamentally atypical and genuinely radical; it is neither simple nor immediately accessible. Konyves' poetry has its roots in the Montreal Jewish tradition, but he very quickly moved out into the dual influences of radical European Modernism of the 1910s and 1920s, and North American video and performance art of the 1970s and 1980s. These contrasting influences certainly make for a unique blend.

Konyves was born in Budapest, Hungary in 1947, and came to Canada in 1956 as a result of the Hungarian Revolution. His family settled in Montreal, where he attended Outremont High School, then moved on to do several years of study at Concordia University (then Sir George Williams). At Concordia he studied with west coast poet George Bowering and east coast poet Richard Sommer. Known as something of an independent in a city noted for its united front literary movements, Konyves was the last poet to join the Vehicle Poets group that congregated around the parallel gallery Vehicle Art in the mid to late seventies (the other members of the group were Endre Farkas, Artie Gold, Claudia Lapp, John McAuley, Stephen Morrissey and Ken Norris). Konyves was instrumental in organizing the projects "poésie en mouvement" (which put poems by 20 English and French poets on Montreal's city buses) and "Art Montreal" (a video cabaret of experimental art that was broadcast on Montreal's cable channel).

Konyves is one of a very few writers in Canada who can be said to have written out of the pataphysical tradition of Alfred Jarry. Although his early work—the largely irrelevant *Love Poems* of 1974—originated out of the romantic lyricism of Leonard

Cohen (an influence that was remarkably prevalent in Montreal during the late sixties and early seventies), under the influence of Vehicle Art and the other Vehicle poets, Konyves was very quick to realign his aesthetics with those of the literary avant garde. His early avant-garde inspirations were found in the writings of Francis Picabia, Tristan Tzara, Hugo Ball, and other Zurich Dadaists. Upon further investigation, Konyves was able to trace the roots of Dadaism back to Alfred Jarry and his pseudo-science of pataphysics. Certainly the work in *No Parking* (1978) and *Poetry in Performance* (1982) is consciously allied with the suppressed avant-garde tradition that originated with Jarry. In allying his aesthetics with those of Jarry, the young Konyves was able to produce a well-reasoned series of highly imaginative works.

In order to discuss Konyves' workings in the realm of pataphysics it would be best to first go back to Jarry for a definition of his created pseudo-science. Jarry defined pataphysics as "the science of imaginary solutions which symbolically attributes the properties of objects, described by their virtuality, to their lineaments" (Jarry, 193). "The science of imaginary solutions" is the way pataphysics has always been understood in the general sense. Jarry, however, was aiming for something a lot more specific in his full definition. I take the second half of his definition to mean that the essential nature of objects (their "virtuality") must be symbolically attributed to their distinctive features or outline (their "lineaments").

Steve McCaffery came close to invoking the essence of pataphysical theory when he quoted de Saussure's formula "Sign=S/s" in his article "Strata and Strategy: Pataphysics in the Poetry of Christopher Dewdney" (191). Jarry's equation of the object in relation to its virtuality and its lineaments comes quite close to de Saussure's definition of the sign being composed of the signifier over the signified. Object and sign, lineaments and signifier, virtuality and signified essentially hold down the same positions in the pataphysical and linguistic equations. McCaffery's idea that, in Dewdney's poetry, the sign is withdrawn (192) parallels Jarry's theory of pataphysics, in that once the virtuality of the object has been symbolically attributed to the object's lineaments, there is no longer any necessity for the object's virtuality to be present. As with Dewdney's language fossils, the virtual has, in part, been absorbed by the lineaments, and the rest is withdrawn.

This linguistic/pataphysical proposition is central to much of Tom Konyves' writing. Certainly it is strongly present in his first significant book, *No Parking*. Consider the poem "Concrete Magnified":

> We approached La Paz with uncertainty.
>
> "Bella, bella" I whispered to the deep night
> just a couple of feet away.
> Her breasts were small, niggardly.
>
> Stationmaster, wood & glass & everything nice &
> the old & the deprived & bowlers in hats & parapluis
> & skin-inspected ivory towers & articles
> of Samoan origin & persuasive irony & Belgrade,
> Tunisia, Corfu. (15)

Whereas McCaffery, in light of his article on Dewdney, would probably say of this poem that the linguistic signs that it presents have had their signifiers withdrawn, I would also maintain that all the virtual properties of the objects in the poem have been attributed to their lineaments. The poem presents us with outline, pattern, design without rational sense; the "message" or "meaning" of the poem has been withheld in the interests of presenting the reader with a pataphysical construct. Even the traditional sense of the "poem" has been undermined and subordinated to the science of pataphysics in this piece.

Konyves' employment of the pataphysical method is everywhere apparent in *No Parking*. Towards the end of the book's title poem there are several somewhat puzzling lines:

> In the middle of things revealed, ships, customs
> houses, elm trees, dakini, *hostie*, Houdini, in-
> spector, window-maker, pasta-maker, cloud-maker... (14)

In one respect it can be argued that Konyves here is presenting a random catalogue of objects, persons, makers; yet that explanation doesn't quite suffice in processing a poem that is, by and large, making sense to a reader. Konyves here is actually offering a "tribute" of sorts to fellow poets Claudia Lapp, Endre Farkas, Ken Norris, Opal L. Nations, Richard Sommer, Artie Gold and Stephen Morrissey, employing a referential system that approaches pataphysics. These writers are identified by distinctive features or lineaments of their writing which become Konyves' way of naming them. Lapp's signifier is the Tibetan goddess Dakini; the Quebec curse "hostie" is a symbolic attribute of Farkas; Houdini of Norris; inspector of Nations; window-maker of Sommer; pasta-maker of Gold; and cloud-maker of Morrissey. Pages could be written to explicate the why or significance of these identifications. Pataphysically, these identifications can be succinctly made in two lines of the poem.

 I have applied the strict definition of pataphysics, as laid out by Jarry, to Konyves' work in order to show how closely to the premises of pataphysics his work often adheres. Jarry himself allowed for a concept of pataphysics that operates in a larger, less precisely defined way:

> It will study the laws which govern exceptions and will explain the universe supplementary to this one; or, less ambitiously, it will describe a universe which one can see—must see perhaps—instead of the traditional one, for the laws discovered in the traditional universe are themselves correlated exceptions, even though frequent, or in any case accidental facts which, reduced to scarcely exceptional exceptions, don't even have the advantage of singularity. (Jarry, 193)

On a less ambitious level, pataphysics allows for a broad range of realities that function as alternatives to the traditional realistic one. In this light, all forms of absurdism and experimental writing can be seen to be essentially pataphysical.

 Pataphysics as a pursuit that "will study the laws which govern exceptions" can again be seen to have a specific bearing upon Konyves' writing. For Konyves the poetical is always an exception and, therefore, pataphysical. In poems from *No Parking* like "I'll Take the Tab" or "The Golden Calf in Technicolor," the world that Konyves presents is totally unidentifiable. At all points these poems are narrated by a "voice of reason"; they are presented as logical constructions even though they make no sense whatsoever on a realistic level. Not only do they present imaginary solutions, they work with completely imaginary facts.

The most significant poem in *No Parking* is the lengthy title poem. A poem of incredible power, "No Parking" is also remarkably illusory. In it Konyves creates an illusion of movement, making the reader feel as if the poem is moving on and on with an increasing propulsion when, in fact, the poem is quite static. When Konyves writes about being "in the middle of things" (9) he is, quite literally, locating the poem. The poem is the middle carved out of the continuity of time. The beginning and the end have been cancelled; the end of the poem is, in fact, a false ending. It is dramatically correct, pataphysically correct, but it doesn't really finalize anything. Konyves cons the reader with the moves of the poem, persuasively leading the reader to a conclusion that is inconclusive. Even he himself, as author, as the voice of the poem, questions the poem's ending. "That's it?" he asks, and the craftsman in him answers, "That's it." (14) In other words, that's all, that's the end of the line.

The poem, as written, is a controlled catalogue, limited and finite, although the form of the poem seems to allow for an almost endless string of images. Once the pataphysical propositions "To die my hair and live again" and "I am / in the middle of things" are established (9), everything is seemingly permitted. But the poem is deliberately limited, reasoned, framed. Ultimately, there is nothing genuinely processual about "No Parking," even although the form of the poem cries process. The great achievement of the poem is in creating the illusion of not being able to find a parking spot in existence as it were, when in actuality the poem is very much parked, placed, located. In this pataphysical construction, Konyves is driving a car that is not in motion, but only pretends to be.

Although Jarry's greatest influence upon the poems in *No Parking* is as a theorist of the pseudo-science of pataphysics, some of Konyves' work emulates a similarity of tone and subject matter to that found in Jarry. For instance, the structure and humour of Konyves' "Peacock" shares much with Jarry's "The Passion Considered as an Uphill Bicycle Race." The blasphemy of Jarry's piece is complemented with equal force by Konyves' surrealistic degrading and distorting of the marriage ceremony.

The humour of this piece is very much an illustration of Jarry's proposition that "laughter is born out of the discovery of the contradictory" (Jarry, 88). The contradictory is certainly at work in the following excerpt from "Peacock":

> The father of the bride is kneeling in front of a great
> polar bear who stands on the altar with a whip, describing
> great arcs and growling...
> The bride suddenly slaps the groom who, shocked, turns around
> and slaps the best man who, shocked, turns around and sees the
> holy archangel hovering 3 feet away from him, waving a huge
> red penis in front of him and winking. (52–53)

The final bringing together of the contradictory takes place in the last lines when "The steeple of the church pierces the full moon til the great / cloud of God descends and covers all amid very loud coughing" (53).

No Parking is an audacious and consciously revolutionary book of poems. Konyves' next book, *Poetry in Performance* (1982) is no less audacious, and quite possibly more genuinely revolutionary. It contains the texts of two poetry collaborations, five "videopoems" (Konyves' term), two poetry performances, a healthy block of visual poetry and four poetics essays. It is a book that is clearly making a statement about the experimental potential for poetry. *Poetry in Performance* is a "large" book, an ambitious book, in every sense, and there are few correlatives to it in Canadian poetry.

In many ways, *Poetry in Performance* is a record of the forces that push the experimental poet to seek his answers and solutions beyond the page. In Konyves' case, we witness his moving into video poetry and performance poetry. Not surprisingly, the roots of this work are strongly embedded in the pataphysical theatre of Alfred Jarry, and the performances and audience provocating of the Zurich Dadaists. For Konyves, it is the work of these writers that serves as a living tradition; he embraces their work as an alternative tradition to the work of the Anglo-

American Modernists. In contrast to the work of Jarry, the Dadaists and the Surrealists, the poetry of the more typically cited Imagists, of Pound and Williams, *does* tend to seem quite tame. In his work Konyves is clearly attempting to build upon the workings of a "wilder" form of Modernism.

"There was a kind of explosion" reads the first sentence of *Poetry in Performance* (1); this is how Konyves describes his becoming aware of Dada. Along with the sense of an alternative to the conservative poetic renovations of Imagism, Dadaism presented Konyves with alternative poetic forms for poetry that enabled him to move beyond the page. The Zurich Dadaists, in particular, were consummate performers. For Konyves they provided a spiritual accessway to simultaneity, collaborative composition and poetry as performance. The work in *Poetry in Performance* is very much rooted in a sense of counter-tradition and artistic community.

The two collaborations that Konyves documents (for the most part written with other Vehicule poets) certainly provide grist for his aesthetic mill, but it is when he moves into the form of "videopoetry" that Konyves really begins to promote his own particular brand of artistic revolt. A videopoem like "Sympathies of War" employs so many of the techniques of the Dadaist and Surrealist repertoire: free association; cut-up texts; dreamlike imagery; suspension of syntax; polyphony; words broken down to their sonic values. As in the texts of *No Parking*, in his videopoems Konyves is primarily concerned with "making sense" poetically, often subverting the rational in order to do so. In "Sympathies of War" he openly employs a language of warfare and conflict within an artistic context. Addressing the title and intention of the piece, Konyves writes:

> What war? The war of spirit and flesh, the war of words and images, the war of literature and the modern medium, video. The war of experimentation and conservatism in poetry, of regionalism and nationalism in society, the war of reward and loss. Sympathy for the imagination at war with rationalism, sympathy for the young who die in war without knowing courage or the instinct to kill. (39)

Certainly this sympathy "for the imagination at war with rationalism" is extended into "Ubu's Blues: The First Voyage of the Vehicle R," the most ambitious piece in *Poetry in Performance*. Whereas "Sympathies of War" is a broken postmodernist soliloquy (a la *Hamlet*), "Ubu's Blues" is a full-fledged absurdist poetry theatre committed to videotape.

"Ubu's Blues" owes much to the work of Alfred Jarry; in it Konyves resurrects the character of Père Ubu immortalized in Jarry's provocative *Ubu Roi*. "Ubu's Blues" can be seen as an extension of Jarry's Ubu play cycle. Konyves' play takes place on the astral plane, which serves as a kind of limbo between earthly existence and the afterlife. It is here that the cowardly and bombastic Ubu comes into contact with the play's other characters: Ponty, General Misunderstanding, Venus and Dada.

The fascinating interplay that takes place between Ubu and Dada can be seen as the dramatic interactions of two theatrical characters; but it is also interesting to view their exchanges as a dialogue taking place between two strong poetic influences. Throughout the play, Dada attempts to incite Ubu to take up arms and to take action. The rather rotund Ubu, however, never even manages to rise to his feet; he lies on his back, on his side, props himself up on one arm, but he never makes it out of a semi-reclining position. In *Poetry in Performance*, Konyves has commented on the roles of Ubu and Dada at length:

> In this scenario, UBU is immobile, paralyzed; perhaps it was a homage to show him thus—that I could not wholly raise him from the dead. But I was quite satisfied to explore what in "Sympathies of War" I referred to as "this half-life". Ubu exuded stillness, a fixedness against which his railing stood in relief. He was a natural for a "poetic" character, given to spewing forth all the venom worthy of the railing Thersites. Having committed numerous atrocities in his lifetime, never with his own hands, going unpunished, dying an ignoble death on the operating table, personified for me a tragic hero of the modern order.
> DADA was the personification of the movement. Finally, in one fell swoop, I would exorcise the spirit of Dada which, to the detriment of my relations with my

friends and other poets, was haunting my every moment of creative composition. It was an opportunity for me to articulate my obsession with this overwhelming force of negation, anarchy, which revolutionized art at the turn of the century in a no less thorough fashion than the industrialization of the previous century revolutionized life, society, in toto. (80)

The emphasis in "Ubu's Blues" is not placed on action of any kind; the poetic dialogue is made to carry the full burden. In many respects, the play is a long meditation upon death. At the play's opening, Ubu recounts the plot against his life that took him out of the world; at play's end he is dead again, having been put, as Ponty states, "back in the book" (99). As are all of the primary texts in *Poetry in Performance*, "Ubu's Blues' is highly imaginative and astoundingly pataphysical.

Poetry in Performance represents a real outer limit in Konyves' work. It is hard to imagine how he could have gone any further in the direction documented in this book. It is, then, no surprise that Konyves' subsequent poetry collection, *Ex Perimeter* (1988), is a lot more seemingly conventional. The poems contained in it are thoughtful in a way Konyves' poetry has never been before. (What's more, they are identifiably "poems," in sharp contrast to the "texts" of *Poetry in Performance* that persistently violate the fixed boundaries of genre.) I believe it is a thoughtfulness that emerges from a poet's silence, and from the fear that he may never again be able to break that silence with marvellous utterance.

At the heart of *Ex Perimeter* is the poem "Ten Poems Around the Block." It is the middle section of the book and it addresses the central issue: what happens when inspiration fails? How can the poet proceed when ecstatic vision and lyrical purity of voice—which constitute the young poet's first plateau—vanish, leaving behind few traces or clues? Confronting this loss, Konyves writes:

There are poems and there are poems,
we used to say, for we were defenders
of the poems, then the guardians of the poems,
and our habits changed and our families grew

until we quite forgot what we were defending
and we secretly relinquished the poem. (28)

As part of a literary movement whose members were quite vocal and active in their twenties, Konyves has seen silence descend upon his own work and upon the work of his friends as they passed through their thirties. Where once he believed he could live in the magical realm of poetry, he has gradually come to realize that everyday life needs to find a way to accommodate poetry; the revolutionary aesthetic he embraced demands that he work out this dilemma at the most fundamental level. "Ten Poems Around the Block" is a fine example of how to pick yourself up and dust yourself off after you've fallen from Mount Olympus:

> The creation of a temporary object, then
> through which a thought flows
> searching for a vantage point
> to view the human soul
>
> preferably with a Canadian theme,
> anything approaching political weather,
> situated with Canadian coordinates,
> intellectual yet familiar, true
> to the moment (33)

There is some dry sarcasm in these lines, but there is also a revelation of the truth. The ten-part sequence addresses the quandary and offers its solution:

> To do as Victor says
>
> write in all the margins
>
> write in between and around the lines
>
> encourage the spirit of Graffiti
> to interfere (34)

These are deceptively simple instructions. To build a viable poetic upon these principles represents an enormous challenge. These instructions also signal a significant shift in Konyves' aesthetics, from a consciously radical avant-garde position (rooted in Jarry and in the Dadaists) to a much more off-handed postmodernism rooted in the literary traditions and social and political realities of contemporary Canada. In *Ex Perimeter*, Konyves effectively buries many of his early influences.

Bracketing "Ten Poems Around the Block" are the sections "The Last Days" (poems of Montreal circa 1979-82) and "Vancouver Poems" (circa 1983-86). "The Last Days" poems exist in a borderland between sadness and mysticism. Every now and again a quirky leap is made, reminiscent of the urban surrealism of *No Parking*, but in these poems the vision is darkening, and the resources available to the poet seem to be diminishing. Anyone who lived as part of the Anglo community in Montreal in the late 70s-early 80s will recognize the ebbing away of cultural confidence that was part and parcel of those times. Many of the poems are small and furtive, on the edge of an imagined underground. Here poetry is almost surreptitious, and even friends (to whom four poems are dedicated) must be referred to only by initials.

The poems in the Vancouver section have a kind of easy openness that easterners envy. As someone *from* the East Coast, Konyves records his personal transformation as he begins to live along the Pacific Rim. There is an "English Bay Vision," and there are "Birds at Qualicum":

> I want my sound to join theirs,
> whether in a shrill ear-piercing cry
> or a soft round whistle
> an ingenious refrain
> or a single pure note—
>
> still my thoughts fly silent
> as the butterfly, and my voice,
> when it escapes, crumbles like earth
> in my fist. (44)

Ex Perimeter is certainly far less "experimental" than *No Parking* and *Poetry in Performance*, but it is also far less predictable than much of the Canadian poetry published in the late 1980s.

The twelve poems offered in the "new poems" (Into This Space) section of this selected offer a smorgasbord of Konyves' techniques and effects. Poems like "Thus Spoke Tzarathustra" and "Motions" emanate from some invisible experimental outpost; "For Leonard" and "Hopscotch" offer a minimalist surrealism. "Around the Point" veers toward domesticity, while "Flamenco" steers a curious course towards Cabalistic mysticism. I sense tentative new beginnings here, especially in pieces like "Into This Space" and the rather poignant "Lost and Found":

> Boy meets dog. Boy loses dog.
> Boy finds god. Boy loses faith.
> Boy finds job. Boy loses job.
> Boy meets girl. Boy loses girl.
> Boy finds freedom. Boy loses innocence.
> Boy finds man. Man loses boy.
> Man finds love. Man loses self.
> Man finds home. Man loses song.
> Man finds children. Man loses wife.
> Man finds gold. Man loses gold.
> Man finds time. Man loses hair.
> Man finds dream. Man loses dream.
> Man finds laughter. Man loses time.
> Man finds meaning to life. Man loses life.

As these new poems demonstrate, Konyves' radical training has certainly stood him in good stead when he has come to write the seemingly more traditionally-based poem. Little of his poetry has ever been offered from any kind of conventional stance or positioning. His body of work is significant and challenging, out of the mainstream and almost out of the blue. I recommend it to you as a splendid refuge from the bland and the predictable.

Ken Norris
August 13, 1995
Toronto

Works Cited

Jarry, Alfred. *Selected Works*. ed. Roger Shattuck and Simon Watson. New York: Grove Press, 1965.

Konyves, Tom. *Ex Perimeter*. Vancouver: The Caitlin Press, 1988.

——. *No Parking*. Montreal: Vehicule Press, 1978.

——. *Poetry in Performance*. Montreal: The Muses' Company, 1982.

McCaffery, Steve. "Strata and Strategy: "Pataphysics in the Poetry of Christopher Dewdney." *North of Intention*. Toronto: Nightwood Editions, 1986.

No Parking

On a Line by Keats

He said
'More'
He said
"More happy love!
"More happy happy love"

And the parking meter above me
turns to Violation.

Opus 7

I remember what no one remembers,
I hear the breathing of skyscrapers and chairs.

There is a girl with patience on her arm.

I have been told
that I gored
a dinosaur
then killed him
then raised him
then killed him again.

On this day
I was innocently involved in a minor accident on 68th Street.
I swear it. May one of the worst judges from the state
hear my confession from my lover's boudoir
where I have been studying the chess that angels play.
                                    We
are not happy together, but we manage.

Wordlessly

wordlessly,
the sun rises, sets, the moon waxes, wanes among
the four mountains of the warrior ants & bees who
ceremoniously appear in two's, three's; bulbous
heat rises from the underground sun of the warrior
moles & goblins.
the have's and the have not's recline on the medieval
couch, exchanging snuff, drinking marinated nectar.
nothing compares.
my love, even, holds her head in her hands.
we caught 2 trout this morning, it will serve us well
when we go down among the cree, she says,
before turning out the light.
I can no longer distinguish the newborn infant's cry
from the lullaby.
bye, bye whispers the lullaby.
by and by echoes the lullaby.
vermin have inhabited heaven since mayday, celebrations,
announcements, activity furious with itself.
Cerberus licks his paw with his middle head.
I have lost the words of my ancestors in one of the
university libraries and no amount of labour will
procure them by Dec. 31.
reality is based upon a legend, which in turn is based
upon sidereal time, which then is stirred in the cauldron
of the void 7 miles east of Granby.
the moustache of my aunt is on the belly of my uncle.
yes, louis, I, too, despair before the inimitable, I,
too, am lazy before the all-expressed.
nothing compares.
the sun rises, sets, the moon waxes, wanes among the
four mountains of the warrior ants & bees who
ceremoniously appear in two's, three's; bulbous heat rises from
the underground sun of the warrior moles and goblins,
wordlessly.

To Dawn

or Just Because the Winner is Always Hiding Inside You
Bless My Soul Mamma You Gotta Know There's Love
in Them There Hills
or To Be Surreal is Difficult Without a Diamond on Your Pinky

Dawn dawn
fifteen layers of sky
peeling sky from sky

The light settles on the bridge of my nose
where the waters of the head are divided
settling like those who invade with snow
those who put out darkness with blue rouge
then all the seasons rush together in a moment

Dawn dawn
sixteen layers of earth
peeling earth from earth

My daughters begin to bleed
volcanos burst from the fingernails of your left hand
right hand left foot right foot

left right left right left right left right
left right left right left right left right
left right left right left right left right
left right left right left right left right left

Lose yourself in the pitch of freedom
and her sister heartbeat
the mantras of trees
the eel of lightning
the dangerous swordfish, erotic
embryotic
with drops from the rainclouds
black with the genes of Chinese monograms

Mr. Morocco draws peppermint flies
moving among them with the ease of a pinball

Mmselle dressed in white
her thighs are white
the light is bright
her smile is right
her soul is tight
all through the night
hermaphrodite
Bite! Bite! Second right!
left right left right

Purple dreams on velvet jeans
The need of needing the one love needed
Indeed, he's bleeding! Watch it! Watch it!
Look out! It's all over my skin!
It's all over my shirt!

Five. represent delineate depict portray picture
photograph snapshot of hot figure and cool shadow
peeling sunfired skin bathing suit set forth figure
describe etc. trace copy mould with back of coal tongs
illustrate symbolize in potash paint etc. charcoal
sculpture etc. engrave blow torch etc.
personate impersonate dust of same dressup
scorched parts of earth colloquial pose as clay actor
act personify play kick ash etc. drama mimic
remnants upon ground etc. imitate

The harmony of dance is pleasing to the eye
The music though sparse is a lullaby

The water is calm, the last wave having rolled into a
bodystocking of sand, warm and arrogant.
I sit in the motorboat watching an angel
land on the opposite shore.
My eye becomes a telescope, the brow an adjustment.
The angel buries a being of similitude.
To put it sharply, but bluntly, no calculations required,
the time has come for all good vehicles
to disappear in the lining of the trousers.
The angel is called Forever and ever Amen.

Suddenly, love.
Suddenly, another crib of warm blood arose on the horizon,
arose so suddenly. How else can you explain the absence
of a good cook? 9-5. Good odds.
Look at these, all busdrivers with gold fillings, taxicab
operators with meters sewn to the backs of their elbows.
I ask you,
enormous disjoined ruminative audience, official membership
by bulk only,
is it not time?

During one brief moment of reflective madness,
pounce upon the great reinforced tyger
and ride to the death!
In the morning, evening fell.

But for a second a flurry of snow.

If there is another way of seeing things, let it be
through the octoscope. I rigged it up to the mast of my
spine until double vision set in, like a pair of rimless puddles.
No sirree, no landlubber can have the faintest. The past
merged with the present so I called them sunny periods,
limited visibility, some rough winds and a mulch of loose
weather.

Watch your watches! Watch it! Watch your wallets!
Deer crossing!
Children crossing!

The annunciation rolled over us, the painting of the lowly
child with goggles, his legs astride a Japanese Honda,
disguised as a straw-laden crib, this was our banner, our faith,
our contemporary belief.

Watch your watches! Watch it! Watch yourself!
Children crossing! Children crossing each other!
Two minutes to dawn. 30 seconds. Five four three two
dawn

Heaven

There used to be nectar
to wash the thoughts free.
Now there's a quota
on nectar, too.

Angels were invisible
now they're building
at the northern gate
you can see them between 9 and 10.

Rebekah

I saw Rebekah approach the well.
in my ears Isaac had begun the afternoon prayer.

Rebekah,
young, her hair pulled tightly back.

An angel came during the night and slew
her father, Bethuel, in divine fashion.

I was sleepwalking among the camels
and they were terribly nervous.

Winter Allegory

Our carriage
                rolls onto the clearing.
On a feather-blanket of snow
                        we ride
huddled together
side by side,
my left hand in hers.

here in the luminous wilderness, among the remains
of a small cottage stands
a burning hearth.

we embrace
the blanket is brown with a floral design.
I can't get enough of her lips.

My Mars is in her Venus, all's well.

Concrete Magnified

We approached La Paz with uncertainty.

"Bella, bella" I whispered to the deep night
just a couple of feet away.
Her breasts were small, niggardly.

Stationmaster, wood & glass & everything nice &
the old & the deprived & bowlers in hats & parapluis
& skin-inspected ivory towers & articles
of Samoan origin & persuasive irony & Belgrade,
Tunisia, Corfu.

I'll Take the Tab

Foolproof.

By virtue of the forementioned, we are pleased.
The pleasure is mine, says the Peach. Allow me, allow me!
Mr. Parakeet & Mrs. Dog share the remains of truth, ethics
& pharmacy. In the name of —! Keep them children
off the streets! Hysteria!

Remember, every broken bottle you see
bears the image of Eternity!
Likewise.

The Golden Calf in Technicolor

Intermediate!
In the massacre it was the chorus
that died, first.

My feet don't stink anymore
since you've sent me that heavenly foot powder.

There is laughter in the halls of Montezuma,
they're drinking vodka on the Volga.

PHOENIX

To burn:
Hera, Demetrius, Veronica, Fletcher, Bozo, Marcel,
Hans, Spitz, Valery, Pushkin, Zahava, Jack.

The sand (Hera) and other raw (Demetrius) materials
are mixed (Veronica) and the batch (Fletcher) is
shoveled (Bozo) into crucibles (Marcel)
in the furnace (Hans) in the evening (Spitz).
The maximum
temperature (Valery) of the molten mass (Pushkin)
1450 degrees (Zahava) Centigrade (Jack), is reached at
  midnight

ART or IF I WERE ONLY IN ENGLAND AND IT WAS 1793

I know I can't draw but
this (finally) sketch
of a boy on a horse
I have drawn them so often
seems a clear photograph.

And that is the meaning of meaning.

Spring or The Premeditated Abduction of Pierre Laporte, Sealed

I came back and it was gone. I followed a trail
of inkspots to a lake not to be sneezed at.

There, to my surprise, the wheelbarrow, rain
beating on it. The white chickens (23)
had long since turned blue, the cup was empty.

You can make all the pronouncements you wish
it's not worth the spool it's threaded on.

The angels sang Holy! Holy!
We killed the winter with snowballs.

Leonard Found Poem 1976

Leonard found a quarter in the yard,
embedded in ice.
He said
"Get something"

I did.

Do Not Be Afraid of Death by Drowning

The deceased had the inclination
to go for long walks at a time.
He did not pontificate, speculate,
inculcate or discriminate.
I hold here his autograph. Notice
how the letters tend to droop.

ON THE SUICIDAL DEATH OF PIERRE PARADIS
OCT. 6, 1975

On the first cut
of the album, right
at the beginning
it's that horn.

Were Men, It Is

A POEM FOR TWO VOICES

were men	it is
themselves, in true	the decibel factor
fashion, accordion	which, when intended to
squeeks and grinding	raise your consciousness
gears and pliers, dividing	above this rational earth
into a thousand little specks	the food of gods spill orgasmic
a rose is a circle, said Max	antibiotic fluid, engendering
in a moment of despair	tiny specks, thousands
a birthright for the wash machine	millions coupling
churning churning silent night	in tens, then hundreds
enfolding this sweet	bullied through mazes
unencroachable vertebra	where the mice had just run
in its grasp, transmutation	over here, under the pond
acceleration, did he not say	first in tens, then hundreds
a soft reaction withers	frogs in brainpower, waves
any 2 out of 3, say one to the left	droves of bees, humming-
of you, the perfect response being	birds, woodpeckers, square
hello daddy dear did you	alabaster, marble stair
perfume the trees in twilight?	falling down, failing down
or engendering tiny specks	floating higher, higher
of purple, careless, free	crashing, they invented the bow
and, moreover, solid, pat	stretching the past
miraculous	miraculously
how each separate thing	as though time had stopped
each moment	on the buses, describing
each unearthed truth	a walnut finish, priced way below
each one of you in your heart	list cost, can diamond rust?
how Jesus in the mercy of his	boneless appetizers made his
virgin bride drips ache	cake seem tasteless, dry
and joy in a brown bag	whether under the weather
lemon gumdrops burst from her	or on top of the ladder
and join in children	joining
sing praise to the lord	necrophilia & pediatrics
hallelujah	birth control & smog control
amen, amen	eastern journey & internal revenue
hear me lord	the fool packing up
angelina	and the judge on goof balls
Hiroshima	interlude of true minds
anathema	impediments

hare krishna
no noxzema
Kharman Ghia
mama mia
all-dressed pizza

bowling shoes and spades
howling on the deck
in moonlight walk-in-river
anachronism of toe-control
harp! harp!

Peacock

I kiss you with the corner of my mouth.

IN THE Holy morning matrimony the priest bends his head
to the bride and places a radio in the groom's vest.
The groom changes to FM and sings along with Bing Crosby's
rendition of White Christmas.
The bride holds green flowers above her head and smiles,
revealing a gold tooth for a left molar.
Her heart is crushed and emptied from a Crackerjack box
by one of the maids in waiting.
The bride covers her eyes.
The groom zips up his fly.
The father of the bride is kneeing in front of a great
polar bear who stands on the altar with a whip, describing
great arcs and growling.
The mother of the bride sits on the lap of the priest.
Her hose is torn above the right ankle
The father of the groom stands outside, his teeth chattering,
freezing in his underwear.
He looks to the left, to the right, between his legs, over
his left shoulder, quickly runs down the thirty steps to the
street, hails a cab, jumps in,
waving a blue flag to the on-lookers.
The bride suddenly slaps the groom who, shocked, turns around
and slaps his best man who, shocked, turns around and sees the
holy archangel hovering 3 feet away from him, waving a huge
red penis in front of him and winking.
The mothers in law faint in unison.
The bride approaches the angel and with each step she melts
until she becomes a gooey mess.
The priest is throwing coins against the altar with the altar
boys who scream and cheer each throw, waving their arms,
rushing to and fro.
The audience begins to leave, throwing jackets, scarves, gloves,
stockings, handkerchiefs, wigs, tophats, watches at the foot
of the groom, who stands with his hands in his pockets, tapping
his foot, as night descends.
The steeple of the church pierces the full moon til the great
cloud of God descends and covers all amid very loud coughing.

Words Can Never Say

Umbrellas hide behind chairs.

How many chickens crossed the road
to get to the other side? Words can never say.

Words can never say, me, I feel like I'm going
out of my mind-house, I'm out of my tree-house,
I'm climbing the walls of my mind, like chalk
on the blackboard, class. Class? Class!

Something words can never say, how I feel blue
hands creeping up my thigh, how blue skies make me feel like
something words can never say.

Warning: health and welfare canada advises that danger

Chemistry and physics are having a sadomasochistic
relationship, chemistry is the guilt of physics,
god knows words can never say.

Danger to health increases,
shadows grow longer with a certain amount
of venus, thick underbrush. Under my thumb,
a stamp, Position Only. If only words could say,
it's quite impossible, there's not a ghost of a chance,
but words can never say.

It's a matter of communication, they say.
What is it? I'm left hanging in mind-air,
followed at night by a large question mark.

No Parking

To die my hair and live again.
I am in the middle of things, yet beginning
over and over
                and over and over. To die
in the middle of things, yet beginning,
over mountains and skyscrapers in the middle
of things, letters, bras, disbursement of money
also that which is paid out, a viking on the waters,
spirit yet beginning, winning, foot by foot,
over and over, in the middle of things, churches,
nightmares, maidenheads, stockings on the dryer,
a kiss from the wall planted squarely on my lips
burning at the stake with onions, to die.

To die, my hair tied to stakes like Gulliver,
stretching from one end of the earth
to the other, my body floating, the sails of the earth.
Ahoy! Ahoy! To die my hair or not to
live again, in the middle of things, the apple-core
of living again, not living again, over and over
hurdles of living again or not living again, yet
beginning

To die my hair and live again. I am
in the middle, between north and south.
North/Alan 3455 Stanley St. 849-8294.
South/Astley 129 Anselme-Lavigne Dollard
des Ormeaux 684-2890 yet beginning, trimming
my hair, just a little off the top please,
leave the ears, I like pony tails,
the silence of airplanes, beached whales. Over
and over, in and out, first slowly, go shallow
then deep, shallow then deep, soft…soft…hard!
round, round, red light! slowly…slowly…yeah,
that's it.

To die my hair is growing long, too
long, too too long, hold it right there, don't
move, just like that, that's it, that's it, that's it.

To die   my hair long, red, white streaks,
too too long, too long, too.

To die in a forest fire, in city hall, in the
evening, quietly, alone, with friends, family clothes,
rags to riches, in a car, in a plane,
in a bird, in a Superman costume, in the middle of the night,
on roller skates, red pavement, begging change,
in a hearse, in an alley, in a soft bed
not of my making, raking leaves in autumn,
smiling at the camera, hold it, just like that,
that's it, hold it, freeze!
Freezing, your arms around me, hugging me,
suffocating, strangled with my own belt,
shot! once, twice, in the head, between the eyes,
right between the eyes, the son of a bitch
shoot him right in the eyes, in the back, shot
in the back, just like that, walking down the street,
minding my own business, when, shot!
in the bathtub, in the hallway, leaning on the glass,
nose pressed to the glass, candy, in a hospital,
nurses smiling, cleaning the bedpans,
of old age, yesterday, suddenly, in my sleep, gone.
In the middle of things, bills unpaid, laundry, coffee,
writing a letter to my congressman, in love,
determined to change watching the river flow
ho ho ho get this, throat slit,
stabbed, over and over and over, watching TV,
just relaxing, watching TV. Poisoned! For what?
I put words in your mouth.
                         To die, in New York,
in Little Rock, in Venezuela, in a canary,
in Kingston, in New York, in California, in Chicago,
in a garage, in India with my guru, in your mouth,
in your cunt, in your ass, in your belly, in your bed,
in your garage, in your living room,
relaxing, watching Mary Hartman, Mary. In Greenwich,
at midnight, in Detroit, in New Orleans, in French,
in Spanish, in Quebec, defending the English
in Toronto, defending poetry,
in Noranda, in Alaska, in debt, in corpus delecti, inverted,
hung, well hung, in a hotel room, in Atlantic City,
under the boardwalk, insensitive, in fact,

run over and over and over, on a highway not far
from here, in a disco, in a disco-bar, in a movie theatre,
smoking dope, shooting horse, Hh, never mind, let things lie,
in the middle of things, yet just beginning, 1901, 1961, 1971,
in a computer riot, in a performance just like this, hold it,
hold it! just like that! That's it!

To die, in Montreal, in Vehicule, on Sunday at 2,
in a McCaffery reading, in a review of my book,
in reply to your letter dated, antedated,
in society, in anti-society, in my underwear,
in a year, inveterate, in confession, in a bathroom
at a party, in art only, in fiction, in a water tank trick,
in diving from a plane, in climbing the impossible mountain
with Julie Andrews, in squinting at the sun,
in a playground, under a see-saw, in my lover's arms,
in my enemy's fort, scalped, dragged away and ravaged
by lions, in the mouth of the Euphrates, in the Nile,
in the Red Sea, in the St. Lawrence,
Superior, eerie. In the inn, having a couple, having
a meal, having multiple sclerosis, having my hair cut.
In a memo to mama. in your station wagon, after the dance,
in a cocktail, in the Star and the Gazette, in the Voice,
in the Times, in the chronicle of our times, in the pride
of my youth, under my skin, in my skiwear,
in my bathing suit, Voodoo! Voodoo!

To die my hair and live again. I am in the middle
of things, yet beginning over and over and over and
over an argument, over a woman, over money, over a
cause, over a right and a wrong, over a game, yet
beginning, learning to say Da Da, moo moo cow,
unlearning horror, Mary. To die my hair and live,
with breasts like pomegranates, a tight ass, a big cock,
a sweet pussy, a lovely face,
over and over, in the morning, in the afternoon,
in the front seat, in the back seat, incognito.
To live again in the middle of things, pastures, a farm,
a penthouse with skylight streaming with the sparkling stars,
overlooking New York, overlooking everything
that has happened between us, yet beginning, a germ
of the universe, a giant among men, distinguished by
a scar on the forehead, a mole above the lip.

To live again, over and over, my soul, wearing jeans and T-shirt,
to attach myself to the infinite typewriter ribbon.

Heaven over and over must be missing an angel,
over and over and over, missing one angel, child, over and over
and over and over, cause you're here with me right now,
sweet little angel, over and over, right now, heaven,
over, your kiss, over, you came COD, over, I'm captured,
over, it's so good, so good, so good, over,
filled with tenderness, over and over.

      Yet beginning, in the
middle of things, which is the fire that emanated
from the celestial fire, when that firmament is illumined
there become revealed four mystical groupings of letters,
each beginning in the middle of things, Mary.
In the middle of things revealed, ships, customs
houses, elm trees, dakini, *hostie*, Houdini,
inspector, window-maker, pasta-maker, cloud-maker,
in the middle yet beginning over and over, to die
and live again, just like that, hold it, freeze!
That's it.   That's it.

POETRY IN PERFORMANCE

SYMPATHIES OF WAR

words magically happily dance between curtains of stop

in the

STOP STOP

in the picture
her maternal instincts are described
before she was betrayed
in the early years of the long war

the walls are splashed with her blood
but her youngest must have her birthday party

STOP

ten candles
one white one black one gray one brown
one red one green one yellow one purple
one blue one

STOP

an anonymous letter arrived in the mail

STOP

in part madame regret inform sympathies of war
lived sword appeal pending testimony major
edward her brother second masonry salvage
active service I know satisfaction many
desirable neutral in the event

STOP STOP

I devote memory memory Carmen children

STOP STOP

race laugh
clowns' chalk
deeper straight
right angles force never
downhill animal circle listened finger held moved father
decoration after if I forget she
punished during swims demanded
in the fog two voices Carmen lucky
feel see smell cannot

STOP STOP

get along built sun
may I be reset to zero after all

STOP

there is a fortune in the lives of men
which belong to us
return it O P unto us
forever now

STOP

black blue green yellow felt pens
sustain our verticals and our horizontals

STOP

anti-life suspended in the gray above our
eyes its cords are spiritlessly tugged by you O P
let go

STOP

when we're upside down turn us rightside up

STOP STOP STOP

must greed object
himself objectionable
gall bladder open closes
closed opens

not room fruits, bricks, pots, lids
open in the middle of words
conceal his visions explicit implicit
anonymous opinion
automatic
stopped the water with wool
some things are clearly stated
intimidated unknown
neighbour without terms
without payment before thirty days
as witness shepherd pasture sheep
put it down

STOP

close the light

STOP STOP

muffle the bell on the animal's neck
that it should not ring

STOP STOP STOP

we take turns
the the burning escape passion

STOP STOP STOP STOP

the the cross miles up trained weather
ever have bronze ever have rose attack frost
looked at
once blind teeth glint raw in the foot every between

the cave is in the mountain
the mountain is in the sickness
the sickness is in the heart
the heart is in the forest
the forest is in the cave I dream of
following the night

in the

STOP STOP

in the last picture she was beginning to smile
her lips were red like fire in the *Time-Life* picture
she was beginning to smile her eyes were blue
like a clear skin in the *Time-Life* picture
she was beginning right foot first
generate sad flowing from her eyes
right hand covers left
but her youngest read braille while we watched her
ward off the angel Death

STOP

a child locked in a room

Yellow Light Blues

based on I Ching, hexagram 30

I

I am standing at the edge of the dark pit, angry
staring down into the black hole where something
is certainly stirring, weeping, holding its sides.
For a long time I was a believer, when I closed my eyes
there was something certainly stilling, weeping.
Now it has become the opposite.

I am standing at the edge of the dark pit,
staring down into the black hole and I know
there is nothing below. A wonderful, full knowing
there is nothing. Like a woman, I have become pregnant
and I have felt it growing in the womb of my mind,
and I couldn't wait.
Now it has become the opposite.

I am standing at the edge of the dark pit,
believing there is nothing and there is no comfort.
I could take all the light of the sun, the planets,
the lamps and fires, squeeze it in my fist
and hurl it down that dark deep pit,
knowing there is nothing there.
Now it has become the opposite.

II

I am only the hunter.
It is early morning, the work begins.
Walking out of the hut lined with snakeskin threads,
knotted cords of parchment,
lineaments of a murky tribal ancestry. The sun
rises high above the mountains, staring directly
into my eyes. My father, my father's fathers
rode upon this land like a pen over paper
designing traps and mazes, water snares
and camouflaged devices, ripping meat apart
with their bare hands, vomiting into clear lakes
under a sun like this.
Now it has become the opposite.

I am standing at the edge of the dark pit
as if I were ensnared in the cords of its darkness,
while my brothers walked along the road above.
It was still early morning. Lean dogs sat scratching their faces
snarling, running and chasing anything that moved,
when the dust-blanket of slow nomads began its invasion
at the edge of town.

Now it has become the opposite.
I am standing at the edge of the dark pit,
clutching a lamp to search out a dried-up well, throwing
stones into the deep hollow. Echoes leap and suddenly
there is something stirring, I'm certain, something caught
in the moment of my looking down. My breath is caught
in the suddenness of recognition
as it flows and floats before me,
drowning infant desires of general knowledge
for I know there is nothing below.

A thick-maned lion growls in some shady grove,
he has not found his way to this pit,
but I have remembered him, my eyes have burned his image
into the rockface until my mouth was stopped
and my reflexes fell. And then a studious sleep
has taken over my senses.
Now it has become the opposite.

III

Now we are two.
Our bayonets are poised and directed toward one another,
fixed like a warrior's gesture in paint, arms raised,
mouth open, inaudible screams pitched into air.
In desperation, I have taken to walking around the pit,
circumscribing with my steps the unholy ground.
My brows are wet, my feet are callused, I will go.

It's only common sense. A line of demarcation,
discrimination, a determining line.

In the first place,
it's the point of least resistance.

In the morning, when the sun's rays break through
the horizon, we will be sitting on a rock in the field,
imagining the roar of lions giving chase,
when an armed convoy starts up the hill
with a spontaneous roar of its engines.
In the same way, the sharp crack of thunder's eclipsed
by murderous cannonfire, the sharp whistling
of bombs over occupied land.

In the second place,
it must be made clear, there's no change
like great change, each day is becoming a revolution
rolling east, drawn to the passive sun.

I couldn't care more.
I couldn't care less.

IV

Of those who were neutral in the revolution, most
have been forgotten. I did not think
they lay unknown in some watery grave
in the Pacific.
The trials were beset by difficulties from the start.
Some of the women stripped themselves from their clothes.
A bloated black youth began to set himself on fire.
It was with such protest that the day broke.
Shops were closed for the observance.
When you and I woke, we were entwined
and I was reminded of another, earlier time.
We were never mentioned by the others.

In the third place,
everything withers and finally dies.
Children run because they must, they run the course
of nature, cannot stop running, climbing on each other,
hurling projectiles and obscenities in the labyrinth of nature.
I have to stop.

V

It is not whether my life's in question
but to what degree my life is in question.
In the fourth place,
you can't keep on doing it and doing it
without some suggestion of the end, an overriding purpose
to it all, a clear outright guarantee of a sort.
Don't imagine.

In the fifth place,
I cannot lay my tears down as quick as my head.
The tide is in, the lovers reunited, yet the cries continue.
And I cannot stop them.

In the sixth place,
Love is at the heart of the matter.
To descend into your warm body
I search out a palace more brilliant than heaven.
It is true we have killed time with our love.

I would never expect it.

VI

The sun, the lightning and the fire have appeared
together in the thunder, lightning and the rain.

The southeast is fading in blue ephemeral light
The southwest is yellow on the infinite plain.

To play out an old theme on her instrument, man
Nature wants to die, so she could be reborn again.

See/Saw

(with Ken Norris)

Cast of Characters

JUSTICE OF THE PIECE
FIRST MATE
2 DANCERS

Scene I

JUSTICE OF THE PIECE

I saw my country in half. broken-hearted, broken-hearted,
marching toward the grave beginnings of an Earned Run
Average, chock-full with servitude, injustice and desertion.

FIRST MATE

Abominable.

JUSTICE OF THE PIECE

I saw my country male and female,
English and French.

FIRST MATE

Master and slave.

JUSTICE OF THE PIECE

I saw my country male and female,
approach the future divorce-minded,
face the firing squad of poverty with fear.
I saw my province pregnant
with power, unilingual, suffering
the alienation of her half-brothers and half-sisters
of the West.

FIRST MATE
Suffer the children…

JUSTICE OF THE PIECE
I saw what might have been, what is,
what will be, periodically cry out
with abduction and murder. I saw
the battle on the plains of Abraham
like I would a balloon.

FIRST MATE
I saw a hundred thousand march to war
on a cloudy day in December, 25 below.

JUSTICE OF THE PIECE
I saw the battle.

FIRST MATE
I saw below the city unfurled
a Registered Retirement Savings Plan,
burrowing its way into the infinite land
of 15 billion dollar programs, to build
an industrial complex at Al Subdil
in the eastern province of Saudi Arabia.
There goes another eastern province.

JUSTICE OF THE PIECE
I saw my sleepwalking country
in a half-way house on Bleury
with a guitar case and a camera.

FIRST MATE
I saw foreign investment
and more foreign investment
and more more foreign investment
settle on the shores of the St. Lawrence
like so many ants on a heap of rotten eggs.

JUSTICE OF THE PIECE
I saw my sleeping country
wake from its deep mediocrity

only to discover a malignant tomorrow
in its left breast. I saw my sleepwalking country
with a guitar case lying open on the sidewalk
on a Saturday afternoon in July; I threw him a dime
to hear him sing of California and the beaches
and the girls with blonde hair and love.

FIRST MATE

He'll cut his hair next week, move back to Ottawa,
think Kaybeck is Kweebeck and opt for Spanish
as a second language.

JUSTICE OF THE PIECE

O Can a dance without partners exist?

FIRST MATE

Merry go round the mountain, merry go round the sky.

JUSTICE OF THE PIECE

I saw the flags waving, I couldn't
help it, I saw the army marching, I couldn't
mistake it, I saw their swords gleaming
bright in the sunlight, I didn't restrain it,
moving with ease and grace
through the crowded streets of my city.
I saw their lips moving
with unmistakeable joual, I couldn't
dig it, I saw the army marching,
I couldn't believe it, I couldn't stop seeing
the merciless merciless hand of fate
pronounce them country and wife,
man and strife, til death do your part...

FIRST MATE

Semen.

The Sign **Anti-** *turns into* **Art** *by obliterating the "−" and the right foot of the letter* "**n**".

Scene II

Two dancers appear

JUSTICE OF THE PIECE
Come, let us make or break a nation.

FIRST MATE
Aren't English and French just made for each other?

JUSTICE OF THE PIECE
Made for washing each other.

FIRST MATE
Made for watching each other washing each other.

JUSTICE OF THE PIECE
I can make out a pair of eyes. What do you make of it?

FIRST MATE
I make it a wrong turn heading down Sherbrooke, going West.

JUSTICE OF THE PIECE
Make yourself comfortable, make room all around,
for a change is being made, a change is being made
all around, change is being made
in nickels and dimes.
What do you make of it?

FIRST MATE
I make it a duet, Francophones dancing
in the streets of Ontario, Grand, de la Savane,
Peel, Fleet, Hochelaga, Galt, Aylmer, Remembrance.

JUSTICE OF THE PIECE
Make yourself believe a change is being made,
make a change by believing a change is being made,
make change happen, one for all—all arms and legs.
What do you make of it?

FIRST MATE

I make it a maple leaf and fleur de lys
as naked lovers, embracing.
I heard someone say, in simultaneous translation,
"love conquers all"
(or was it just the daily shifting of earwax)

JUSTICE OF THE PIECE

There! is emotion excited by a novel,
unexpected thing; there is astonishment
mixed with perplexity, curiosity
and there, in the second row, yes,
admiration. I should not be surprised.

FIRST MATE

Faisons-le avec Mary. Faisons-le
avec Janey and Mary. Faisons-le avec Mary,
et Merle, Jacques et Patricia, Marcel, Jennifer, René.
Faisons-le bien.

JUSTICE OF THE PIECE

What do you make of the act of interfering
unlawfully, in a suit, by making
a financial contribution to either party, to carry it on?
What do you make of that? Let's make a rule.

FIRST MATE

Pack your suitcase and head for Toronto.
How do you make a fortune?

JUSTICE OF THE PIECE

You make a fortune by making war. Make war
against the disease of language and culture
threatening our suburbs, infiltrating its hideous thoughts
thru TV… now only 9.99!

FIRST MATE

You can make the team by swallowing goldfish
followed by an infinitive. If you watch your watch
you can make the train behave.

JUSTICE OF THE PIECE
Make the train behave, by making
500 miles the first day, and so on.

FIRST MATE
So, on the train, make the goldfish behave.

JUSTICE OF THE PIECE
By following them with an imperative.

FIRST MATE
Let's make it with Janey. Let's make it
with Janey and Mary.

JUSTICE OF THE PIECE
Let's make it good. Make an oath.

FIRST MATE
Maudit parapluie, if it ever stops raining
I'm gonna stomp those Mae Wests in the gutter, I swear,
maudit tabernacle, shit, I swear,
by the power invested in this paradise, on becoming
a disabled veteran of the force of good, fuck!
I swear, Big John, if we ever get outathis alive,
we'll have the sheriff's head! and then some, too…

JUSTICE OF THE PIECE
The white paper has become the blueprint
we will never forget. War, we will never forget.
War, we will never regret.

FIRST MATE
If this is the second movement, like
1st, 2nd, 3rd, bearing in mind
the elemental nature of the piece, first,
why can't we just say so? I mean,
war, we will never forget, a wart
we will never forget. But who is
Peter Paul Van Kemp?

JUSTICE OF THE PIECE

Make merry, my friends, make haste, mes amis,
for the bell is struck in our land; the crickets' chirp
has stopped, and the machine has gone full tilt.
What do you make of it?

FIRST MATE

It's a Bell Canada bill, made out to monsieur,
a little love note from the tele-boutique.

JUSTICE OF THE PIECE

Make believe that this is not happening,
not here, not now, not ever, not to you,
not to me, not to him, not to her, whether
we like it, or not. What do you make of it?

FIRST MATE

A frog fable. One day,
I came upon this frog in the elevator,
1st, 2nd, 3rd, 4th, 5th,
on the 6th, 7th, 8th, on the 9th
of December, I think it was.

Scene III

The Sign **Anti-Country** *turns into* **Art-Court** *by obliterating the "i" and "y" and the right foot of the two letters "n".*

JUSTICE OF THE PIECE
French schools or English schools?

FIRST MATE
School English schoolchildren in French schools.

JUSTICE OF THE PIECE
School French schoolchildren in English schools.

FIRST MATE
School English schoolchildren in English schools.

JUSTICE OF THE PIECE
School French schoolchildren in French schools.

FIRST MATE
School immigrant schoolchildren in French schools.

JUSTICE OF THE PIECE
School immigrant schoolchildren in English schools.

FIRST MATE
School children of immigrant schoolchildren in French schools.

JUSTICE OF THE PIECE
School the nieces of immigrant schoolchildren in English schools.

FIRST MATE
School the famous children of immigrant schoolchildren in French schools.

JUSTICE OF THE PIECE
School the children of immigrant schoolchildren
in ways to make them vote for French schools for
English schoolchildren, or children
of immigrant schoolchildren, socialization,
disestablishmentarianism, depotism,
fear of science and unidentified material phenomena,
boxing games.

Scene IV

JUSTICE OF THE PIECE
In the north and northwest, the winters are long
and harsh, the summers short and hot.
Winter arrives early and is followed by
a late spring and hot summer. L'Annonciation.

FIRST MATE
Halifax.

JUSTICE OF THE PIECE
Musquaro.

FIRST MATE
Corner Brook.

JUSTICE OF THE PIECE
Joliette. Rimouski.

FIRST MATE
It was like a nightmare. One minute, we were talking,
the next, there was a crash. I wasn't looking at her.
I was driving.

JUSTICE OF THE PIECE
Temiscaming.

FIRST MATE
I was watching the road.

JUSTICE OF THE PIECE
Gagnon. Grandes Bergeronnes. St. Tite.

FIRST MATE
I looked over and saw… looked over and saw…

JUSTICE OF THE PIECE
Lachute.

FIRST MATE
This hole in the windshield.

JUSTICE OF THE PIECE
Laval.

FIRST MATE
She was covered with broken glass...

JUSTICE OF THE PIECE
Langlade. Latuque. La Reine.

FIRST MATE
Bleeding... The rock smashed into the windshield, shattering it, smashed into her stomach, at 4:05 p.m.

JUSTICE OF THE PIECE
Bale Comeau.

FIRST MATE
The rock came off the bridge, about 15 feet above the highway.

JUSTICE OF THE PIECE
Chibougamou.

FIRST MATE
Whether it fell of its...

JUSTICE OF THE PIECE
Sherbrooke. Magog.

FIRST MATE
We both work at the psychiatric hospital.

JUSTICE OF THE PIECE
Sept Iles. Québec.

FIRST MATE

In a similar incident, a 64-year-old woman
was killed by an 80-lb. boulder, dropped from an overpass,
by a 15-year-old boy.

JUSTICE OF THE PIECE

Mont Jacques Cartier. Mont Louis. Mont Tremblant.
Mont Laurier. Monet.

FIRST MATE

Two boys, believed to be 12-14 years old,
were seen carrying a 30-lb. cobblestone,
during the rush hour.

JUSTICE OF THE PIECE

Ste. Marie. St. Sauveur. St. Jérome. St. Jean.
St. Jovite. St. Gabriel. Ste. Agathe. St. Lin.
St. Germaine. St. Georges. St. Pamphile.
St. Pascale. St. Jean Port Jolie. St. Simeon. Ste. Anne.
Ste. Augustine. St. Pierre. St. Paul.
St. Profond d'en Arrière, St. Félicien. Ste. Hyacinth.
St. Joseph, mon dieu.

FIRST MATE

Tuesday afternoon.

JUSTICE OF THE PIECE

Montréal. Montreal.

The End

Ubu's Blues or The First Voyage of the Vehicle R

Across the foliated space of the twenty-seven equivalents, Faustroll conjured up into the third dimension:
   From Beaudelaire...
   From Bergerac...
   From Luke...
   From Rabelais...
   From Ubu Roi, the fifth letter of the first word of the first act.

—Alfred Jarry's Doctor Faustroll, Pataphysician, chapter 7

Cast of Characters
UBU .... *reincarnate, rotund, reclining or sitting throughout*
DADA .... *the fool, with goggles and a long pointed nose*
PONTY .... *the author*
GENERAL MISUNDERSTANDING .... *a child of 7*
VENUS .... *the love element*

Scene I

UBU

Merd*r*e!

DADA

Occult lore has it that man has (a) an astral body and (b) a physical body. Under certain conditions, they may separate, with the consciousness accompanying the astral body. We refer to this experience as astral projection. A silver cord is said to link the astral and the physical. Some even go so far as to say that if the cord is broken, death will result. Ubu, eternally at war with the reasonable, has been astrally projected on to this dream machine he will only know as the Vehicle R.

PONTY

(taps Ubu's forehead once)
Ubu!
(No response. Taps Ubu's forehead again)
Ubu!
(No response. Taps Ubu's forehead a third time)

Ubu!
(Ubu opens his eyes)

B is for…

PONTY

Birch.

PONTY

Once there was a brave king…

UBU

… murdered in his bed by his trusted servant. A good king. A brave king. *(Thunderous knocking)* My sword! My guards! My servants! We are not… We have to be… And you, sir, are not the least bit of assistance to our royal insubstantial self. The collège of 'pataphysique will hear about this, we assure you!

PONTY

(Opens door) Hello? Why… there's nothing below! Ubu!

UBU

What is it?

PONTY

Ubu… we're… on the air!

Scene II

UBU

We were prepared to die at the end of October, November, nineteen hundred seven, the butler had done me in, in the worst way, in the fourth hour of the imperial day, in our bedchamber; I was accosting some faceless wench in our royal slumber, when this…this base parasite of our orifice extended the garden shears to dismember this royal flesh.

DADA

The peritineal cavity is opened, and the point at which the stomach is to be incised decided upon.

UBU

He was determined to stick me to heaven.

DADA

The stomach is now opened by a transverse incision and the foreign body extracted.

UBU

Like a foreign wild boar, I roared *(in a tiny voice)* "Help me, help our person…" *(growling)* I will have revenge! I will not be ground up and served to swine, I have the divine right and left to live… I came not naked into this high oriffice!

DADA

The incision is commenced opposite the eighth intercostal space, two inches from the median line, carried downward for three inches. Haha!

Scene III

Ubu, at the foot of Venus.

UBU

Aroma of Roma, hyacinth! A wreath for the dead. Who cares for Ubu, now that he's dead? The filthy poverty of it all! Alfred, they will have your blood! Foul stench! Embalm poor Ubu, will they? Where have all the flowers gone? Sweet Venus, is that you?

VENUS

Orientals are more than usually sensitive to the offensive smells of their climate, Ubu. I am at the bottom of a narrow well... well, looking up. I reach out to the sides and I can touch the two sides; a slippery wet wall on my left, a dry rock wall on my right.

UBU

The river Styx.

VENUS

A thick liquid oozes down my arm, warm, like blood, Ubu.

UBU

I am a fossil of life, no more.

VENUS

It's oozing down my leg now, feel it. Warm blood of flesh... desire.

UBU

A great invention, life.

Scene IV

DADA

I see myself in you,
going up, going down,
I am rushing to the head,
I am russian to the toe.
I go one step up,
I go one step down;
if you think different,
watch this frown.

Ubu, you... be... you?

UBU

I must be sick in death to see such awful visions. Busy, busy, burdens on our backs, bonnets on bonnies, babes in babels, baggage, banged like the woman of Bath, badgered on the balcony of crime, baked bacteria.

DADA

Bad man!

UBU

Backsliding mortal bowels of men, a baroque brigade, we...

DADA

(wheezing) Weeeee...

UBU

... marching, marching, then, there! a barricade! We...

DADA

(wheezing) Weeeee...

UBU

... the barbed barbarians! We...

DADA

(wheezing) Weeeee...

UBU

… base batch for a battle, burning inside our brains for blood. Burning thirst for blood! We…

DADA

(wheezing) Weeeee…

UBU

… bent over bodies, charcoal flesh, a feast for the beasts—my head is like a billiard ball… potted. Beggary! We…

DADA

(wheezing) Weeeee…

UBU

… we beggar army, our bellies full of snow, brother eats brother… Bells! Bells! Bells! Beware of bells, clown. The skies blacken, the voices of sheep bleating baa-baa, poor bastards, blindfolded from birth, poor bastards, one brief peek at beauty, then… BAM! Blown to bits! Boils! Body-snatcher, what boredom are we now subjected to?

DADA

A bouncing box, a bottomless well, a brave deed, indeed. Ubu, if you be you, you'd be better off… And now, it's time to explode a myth, unearth the truth, drive home a point, flush out the little rascal, expose, spell out, elucidate and unravel the mystery…
There once was a once-was that was once,
a once-was that was once a was-once,
when was-once that once
that once-was that once
that once was a was-once once twice.

Scene V

GENERAL MISUNDERSTANDING

Stop! Nancy says it's not all right! *(draws his sword)* Nancy says it's not all right, and that is that!

DADA

He calls after her: I'm on my enemy's heels, I've caught him, I've caught myself in the act, I can't remember, I won't be held responsible, I won't be held! Hell! Just a couple of a more days, a few weeks was all I needed, and her bedroom manner… can I get you this, can I get up for just one minute… One thing has nothing to do with the other, what was once that life is this life, what was once that death is now this death. I would have given you the shirt off my back, back then, it wasn't so easy. I don't care what you say, you can give it to me or give it to your country. You have a wife who calls your name, then coughs herself to sleep, to dream of dolls, immutables, a kerchief, an arm on the bus, beep beep, boopety boop, boppety bop, hopscotch here from 1 to 3 then 2 to 5, 6, 7, 8, 9, 10. Then back again, 10, 9, 8, 7, 6, 5, 4, 3, 2, 1…

GENERAL MISUNDERSTANDING

Blastoff! Hubert Edmund Blastoff, octogenarian, subject to falls and a rarely heard scream, in desperation denies home, family, material gain, poetry of substance, comings and goings, eat, sleep, swim, dream…

DADA

Skin team, eat, sleep, weep. First you weep, then you reap. Where do you belong? Belong in coming and going. Father of fear of fear itself, who inspireth in us to fear the next turn around the corner in us, inspireth dreams in us to be there, not be there. It's all a bunch of rubbish, trash. It's all a bunch of roses, she laughed and laughed, kissed away her education with a flip of a coin, o how we laughed on the night we woke up to mice in the field where once we had run. Where once we toiled the soil, we now soil the oil. We sow discontent among the simple folk. Their mouths are watering, their eyes are burning with both hate and love, half wanting to just get on with it, line it up, shoot it down, so the blood is the colour of the roses in her cheek, the darling… six years old and a smile to win a war.

GENERAL MISUNDERSTANDING

Love and money, that's what it's all about, kissing, drinking, taking it off the wall, putting it back again, peeling eggs and potatoes, being true to one, not the other.

DADA

That's a dog of an idea, General. Now, who goes first? Who gets to the smooth skin of things…

GENERAL MISUNDERSTANDING

(To the tune of Mickey Mouse …) U-B-U, U-B-U, U-B-U-B-U.

DADA

Eggs and potatoes? Onions and pears? This man's life is in question, or should we say, the degree to which his life is in question has never been satisfactorily answered.

GENERAL MISUNDERSTANDING

I think you are making sense, Dada. A few cents here, a few cents there, it all adds up, Dada.

DADA

What do you know?

GENERAL MISUNDERSTANDING

I was on an island, surrounded by wild animals, tigers, bears, lions, snakes. A dinosaur or two. Birds with wings as long as rivers, necks thick like trees. But I was not alone.

Scene VI

PONTY

Well, this is it.

VENUS

What is it?

DADA

Is what? Is what?

PONTY

Nancy says it just won't do, the whole thing is off. There's no money for us to get paid for what we do, the whole thing has turned her off, she says everyone to just go one home and forget it.

DADA

What do you mean, forget it?

PONTY

Ubu has to go back in the book. That's all. Enough play.

GENERAL MISUNDERSTANDING

What do you mean, enough play? The sunlamp…

UBU

We did not find you entertaining in the least. Your sal-on manners leave nothing to the imagination and, really, what the good lord intended for us to have, he gave, and plentifully.

DADA

Isn't that blue-tiful?

VENUS

Who cares for Ubu, now that he's dead?

GENERAL MISUNDERSTANDING

Consult the alphabet, dear. If I'm not mistaken, it's a miniature. The souls of these men have gone into dolls, no return bottles.

VENUS

A message in the bottle floating through the sea of time: My dearest love…

DADA

STOP!

VENUS

Dearest love, will you…

DADA

STOP!

VENUS

My dearest angels, lay your heads on my feet, you shall be comforted, and plentifully.

DADA

Alfred Jarry was born in two different cities. The letter which attests to this fact is the letter R. Alfredo invents a myth while drinking wine. The symbol: a rose by any other name should begin with the letter R. Hung by the neck till he was dead. Till he was dead, till he fell down dead. Till he was dead, till he felldowndead.

PONTY

If I struck his head three times, I struck it a hundred times. No sign. No sign of life there at all. His body was… deserted. I called out, UBU! like that, three times each time. But it was like talking to a wall… through a wall.

The End

Ex Perimeter

Montreal Lane Vision

A couple of clothespins later
another creak
the cat looks up
in heat: a sunbather looks down
in between the leafy branches
where the sparrow turns and spies its mate.

And it's these sparrows
who repeat all our thoughts
in their infernal dialogues
their gossip not meant for us
watching rainbuckets mirror
the stately Versailles.

The Leaves in November

The leaves in November
twinkle like damned stars.

You say
I do not wish to deceive you
and if it wasn't for your smile
I'd believe you

I don't want to paint you
I'm no painter

The Last Days

Head tilted north
mouth wide open
she is prepared
to receive the spirit
who must finally take pity
and descend
into her being
and extinguish the flame there
and light another
for eternity

The Funeral

I am not permitted in the funeral hall,
I sit in the car, listening to the CBC
two days after the election
of another government, I watch them load
the casket covered with a black shroud,
its Hebrew inscription:
The law of the Lord is perfect
restoring the soul.

I am not permitted in the cemetery,
I sit in the car, sighing heavily.
My father:
"Today is our 34th wedding anniversary.
This is a gift for our suffering
with her, three of us feeding her
every day for eleven months."

The bulldozer driver pauses for a cigarette.
The next fill is not due for an hour.

At the Pik-Nik

Behind the counter, she serves
as a symbol. A red and white
baseball cap to match her white shoes,
red dress. She's about seven months pregnant,
speaks French to all her English customers.

The danish sits, anticipating a purchase
like a subdued puppy in a pet shop window.
A display case opens, mounted on the wall.
"Today's her birthday, how old
do you think she is?" chats her identical twin.

"She's the queen of milkshakes," I tell her,
thinking
Poetry to you dear S
is an elastic band
around the coffee sticks.

To L.D.

L.D. is looking for thinkers —
not voyeurs and witnesses
to life's slow turns
and frozen images.

He needs these poet-thinkers
like a mother her infant's cry;
but he wants the poet-rebels
like a young man thirsts for ale and flesh.

Hallowe'en

Halloween means caution
evil lurks in every treat
in every bag: like razor blade apples
and LSD candies, poisoned gum
and ink-filled prunes, spider pies
and black-fly brownies, zombie
fingers, goblin goo, kid-
nappings, murders! tortures!
cries of ghosts in chains
as blood like a snake
slides silently downstairs

A night when evil meets Evil
and discovers it's a joke.

CHRISTMAS EVE 1980

Christmas Eve and it's raining
reindeer, a Santa-clone appears
with needle trees and coloured bulbs:
the night is silent, if not holy.

Jingle bells are tolling,
the New Year's rolling in—
end of a decade. A merchant
neon-lights his window: PEACE SVP

To New York

Of course I'm not happy that three times
I've come to you and three times
I've been a victim of leaving my car unattended too long
too romantic in this
City of giants, city of ants
I speed up and down your red middle east avenues
I maneuver stealthily through your streets of eccentricity
I'm not here for your Folk City annual
Bob Dylan sound-alike contest
Hello? Sami Beckett here, got a play opening off-Broadway,
off 8th Avenue, on 42nd.
Wait for me in front of the Clurman.
The street is my ashtray, I shall not want for expired students,
gang-bang orangutans, yippies chanting
"no nukes, no narks, no nations,
bring that warmongin' son of a bitch Reagan to his knees"

My pigeons are heroic bombers in the dawn's early light
(knock knock) Who's there, there? Readers. Readers? Who?
Readers who are sprinkled beside the baseball
diamonds in Central Park,
carriers of 21st century diseases, meet
mace-in-the-face gangs, who
terrorize windshields with wet rags and bones for fingers,
just depress lever against them.
What a catastrophe of capitalism.

It takes four white policemen, five white policemen with bats,
six white policemen with guns,
seven white policemen with sirens
wailing the Columbus Avenue blues,
to subdue a resisting black woman in white shorts,
twist her wrists with crooked hands–
Let us make man in the image of this city.

You just can't get a better deal, he confessed,
make a hundred thousand
nylon wristbands with zippers (for cash and keys)
at a dollar forty, retails at seven dollars,
Walter J. Thompson's interested,
Club Med will pick up fifty thousand,

Kellogg's is interested, get it? It could be a coupon prize,
so, what d'you say?
Want a pickle? no charge, there you go. Have a nice day.

Pick the red. Put your money down. Everybody wins.
Try your luck, sir, no money down.
The comer of the red card is curled.
I decide to turn up a black. "He's blind," they cry.

It's a perfect night on Flatbush Avenue,
coming off the Manhattan Bridge
"does she need me like she pretends"
Tonight Marlene will sleep on the carpet in her sleeping bag
and not being able to sleep will lie next to me
not being able to make love to her.
I regret not staying up all night with her,
kicking cans down 6th Avenue,
singing love songs, reading two-day-old newspapers
in allnight restaurants
with salsa pulsating through the air-conditioned air.

Ten Poems Around the Block

1

Unblock a wave of words for him
for he suffers
from a respiratory ailment

Unlock a chamber of wild thoughts for him
or any thoughts but these
morning exercises

Excuse him for doing nothing
but in his secret heart to dare
the world to open
like a book

A friend stands in front of the lens
challenging, "Take it!
Take it, now!"

2

I remember how the bricks of the old building
inspired nothing
how young trees moved about in creaking art galleries
and you sat pensive but writing with your left hand
into a notebook of love poems which we shared
until there was nothing and suddenly no meaning
in a common mirror and how I boasted in French
c'est le bon dieu and let the pen fall

3

Atop the Mayan ruin at Coba
where the jungle stretches to the horizon
in every direction

a perfection seized him
without a reflection
he could translate
and pocket

He became the ghost atop Coba
distracted by circling wasps
and the heat of the moment
that dumb eternal moment

4

There are poems and there are poems,
we used to say, for we were defenders
of the poems, then the guardians of the poems,
and our habits changed and our families grew
until we quite forgot what we were defending
and we secretly relinquished the poem

and it would reappear from time to time
to haunt us with an opening line
or a curious concern and I would say to you
I remember that and what could we have been thinking
not to sit and write on
when you replied
just taking it day by day

5

Another blank page
for an empty pen
to tap

and you insist on tempering beauty
with domestic utility

It's in savoring your sweet lips
that hope succeeds and speaks
in poetry

how do you justify
not holding still

6

As it turns out
it's not the step
into the arena
with THE DEVOURER

As it turns out
the poem is the step
out of the arena
into the real
where we are separate
mortal gristle

7

Eye to eye, is it?

A father to rebel against?
A teacher to reeducate?
A critic to feast?
A poet to mystify?
A lover on a bed of roses?

This muse has no tongue
her breasts are empty
her fists are clenched

8

1 have not always wanted to read them
outloud, and I never wanted to introduce them, in fact
they belonged to someone else
who held them sacred and who was I

to introduce them, in fact
reminded me of english lit classes
and bells ringing
at the most inopportune moment

regard sacred the mischief of my mind
I wanted to say to them
when the black cape was in the air
and in their notebooks
the date was preceded
by the day of the week
then course number, decimal, number

a part of me always wanted
to be somewhere else
chasing words around furniture
around the listening moon
and it was this part
I miss most

9

The creation of a temporary object, then
through which a thought flows
searching for a vantage point
to view the human soul

preferably with a Canadian theme,
anything approaching political weather,
situated with Canadian coordinates,
intellectual yet familiar, true
to the moment

10

To do as Victor says:

write in all the margins

write in between and around the lines

encourage the spirit of Graffiti
to interfere

Approaching Guerrillas

Read a hundred poems
and you still question why
the killer beast so survives
in the imagination, why
generations of experience
cannot seem to teach plain tolerance

why children end up dying
at the hands of their fathers and mothers,
why peoples starve while others cruise
in space, why all these poets
yearn for visions while reporters
are shot in the doorway of a church.

My Dear Mary

I have started writing again
imitating the lights strung
across tennis courts:
to dance the last dance of fall.

My horoscope's recommending
fundamental changes, urgent
hypotheses:
"create order where there's disorder now"
and
"succeed where others fail"
or
"carnal love intervenes"

Vancouver Rag

Joggers brush past me around Stanley Park,
smiling. I can't figure it out,
in a historical sense. Beardless,
the sunlit profile threatens to wash it all away
into the blue-black sea. On the right,
on the highway, a black vulture glides to a stop
just as the radio announces:
The Leader of the Opposition
has just been forcibly removed
from the House (and into the arms
of the Station Manager, generating
a controversial talk-show host).

How cosmopolitan! Surrounded by oil portraits
of dogs, Chinese cabinets, porcelain turkeys,
brass candlesticks and urns demanding
a pastoral trio to work the fading garden,
garbed in silk, a subtle silver chain in tow.

I separate myself from my work,
walk down to the beach
with mindless desire for the remote mountains
where my words turn to desperate prayer
and my body to a glowing meteor.

English Bay Vision

There is no futility in commerce, not here
in the land of abundant symmetrical logs
on manicured beaches

A warm summer wind blows flags for fun
and in every shake a substitute
for the tragic poem
which eludes me here
I cannot complain:
the mountains stare down

Our heroes are born infirm
or destitute
the same old anti-nuclear protest echoes
in this mirrorless garden, Beauty dances
with a sandwich sign
an artifact
a tattoo

Birds at Qualicum

I want my sound to join theirs,
whether in a shrill ear-piercing cry
or a soft round whistle
an ingenious refrain
or a single pure note —

still my thoughts fly silent
as the butterfly and my voice,
when it escapes, crumbles like earth
in my fist.
             It's not
that I want to be like them
in some anthropomorphic death wish —
it is the ever-circling breeze of living
in the grace of space.

Their endless variations
as monotonous as my breathing

I sense a glacier moving back and forth
between continents

On the Birth of Alexander

For months
I felt his pushing
against the womb;
I rubbed Marlene's belly
like a magic wok
wondering
who's being born,
into what world,
from which page of our dreams
onto this hospital bed.

For hours
Marlene struggled
with the Invisible Creator;
she shook her body
in his face,
all our eyes
fixed on a fragile head
plucked and tugged into the light.

All the wonder
of a walk in the rosegarden
in moonlight, our eyes
fixed on each other,
hearts one

Four Quarts

for Duane and Arthur

1   You who lie now silent in the perfect deep
         be refreshed by these thoughts of you
         walking in the wind with violet flowers
         toward the end of summer, '72.

         Illuminate the wood with your burning spirit!
         Dance on the leaves! Swim in a river of light!
         Behold the beauty of snow
         on a braking blue train!

         The neck of your guitar still buzzes
         to young girls who sway, whispering
         "honey" and "love"
         though all you ever sing of
         is spending your last dollar
         standing under the red light
         weeping in the blue rain.

2   Lord Lord have mercy
         you know what I mean
         bend that string around my brain
         tune me out of my misery

         Yes I'm ready for you
         on a wild ride through the clouds
         spitting out the answers
         in a demonic A

         the D being the cradle,
         the E being the grave.

3   In memory of Elizabeth
    who may have climbed a wooden staircase
    with golden-haired Michael at her side
    I see her conducting a celestial number
    from a candle-lit house on a farm
    where Ginsberg's horses are uncommonly dark
    and the fields are lonely and grey.

4   I was never one for turning back
    turning my back on the present full moon
    bright at two o'clock in the star-filled sky —
    what fortunate meeting! expressed more now
    in death than anguished friends
    who meet in shade and tip their hats:
    Good morning, brother Duane!
    Good evening, brother Arthur!

A Vision of Bureaucracy, After Kafka

We thought we knew
and we did
until we didn't know anymore.

Only they knew.
(If they didn't, we had no idea.)

One afternoon, we were certain we knew.
They rushed in with the news. We
couldn't have been happier.
We finally knew.

It was like an orgasm.

The next day it rained. Suddenly,
we were alone. Suddenly, we didn't know
anymore. Again,
only they knew.

They said they didn't know,
but by this time
we didn't believe them.

We knew
they knew.

The Tree of Singing Birds

On Dias de las Muertas
the sacred day of remembrance
bright red long-stemmed flowers appeared
bright orange flowers with yellow petals
appeared, trails of petals to every corner,
church bells call
as hundreds of birds
converge on the square
to the tree of the square
the tree of singing birds

how it endures the lone violin
and the silent stroke of my pen

INTO THIS SPACE

Thus Spoke Tzarathustra

"It is indeed better to live among hermits and goatherds than among our gilded, false, painted mob—even if they call themselves 'good society'"

Zarathustra

"After all, everyone dances to his own personal boomboom, and the writer is entitled to his boomboom: the satisfaction of pathological curiosity; a private bell for inexplicable needs; a bath; pecuniary difficulties; a stomach with repercussions in life; the authority of the mystic wand formulated as the bouquet of a phantom orchestra..."

Tristan Tzara

Not in my right mind, that is to say, poetically,
I awoke today from a dream of thirty-three years.

I was hungry, but I was not fed; I loved
but I was not loved. I was prey to the rich,
scorned by the poor; what I built was destroyed,
what I tore down was resurrected.
I found my soul in the darkness
when my spirit fled. I repented
but was never forgiven. I prayed
but only an echo returned to me.
My heart stopped beating
but I did not die.

Windshield wipers sway and dance while pistons of war collide,
rattling like a one-armed bandit
in this pressure chamber of a world.

The road to the mountain passes the cemetery.
You see, you see, you see, you see, goes the needle
at the end of the record.
I lie (I lie) sideways on the bed,
my hands and feet hang over the edge,
white chargers race across a blackboard,
German tanks and British warships
roll and weave across the screen.

There must be a misunderstanding. Notions
of propriety, decency, all that is upstanding and right,
generous, pleasant giddy-ups of good
have invaded my little world.
I came here not well, parading a tired lion
in the streets of the capital.
We have been playing a charade
of no consequence, Empires Are Falling:

the terrier chases
the fox in the hole,
the leopard leaps
from the tree.

I will change, I will change,
I will whip the new left with traditional chains.
What could be worse than not being listed
in the Canadian Book of New Penguin Verse?

I will rhyme, recall the solitude of wax heroes,
serve Pan and the insects, I will question
every natural event (beasts propagating
allegorizing my lusty adventures)

I brace myself for one more leap
then out I fly in the twisting air
somersaulting silent clouds,
screaming below Doo-Da! Doo-Da!

Thus spoke Tzarathustra.

BLUES AT THE RISING SUN

she's my sweet little thing, he groans
heads nod
feet tap

because
she left him
and he's gonna kill anyone
who messes with her

you don't come between
the sweet little thing
and her lover boy
if you know what's good for you

inevitably
someone comes along
to warm her heart
and steam her loins

someone
you could never know
you don't even want to know
his name

he changes her
every time he looks at her
he raises her on his wings
into the warm summer sky

while you stand
in the frozen storm
ringing the bell
hammering on the door

across town she's yelling
at her 3-year-old daughter
give back the man his money
he just laughs and says that's all right honey

you just keep the money, go
get yourself a doll
and leans back on the sofa,
settling in for the night

blow smoke rings at the light
the night and the blues
check out the girl
with the frizzy hair

this is all about
how everybody needs
some kind of insurance policy
because you never know what's coming down

down the stairs
she flips her hair
throws back her head
and sways to her seat

bouncing hips
and confidence
shakes her head
when asked a question

culture shock
for the girl
from Defiance, Ohio
this is mojo country

I'm everything
to everybody
I snap my fingers
you feel the pain

baby! baby!
baby! baby!

I want to pick you up in my arms
and whirl you around the dance floor
your face
the face of every woman I loved

and still you
and your warm breath on my neck
and the lights in your eyes shine red
like the rising sun

[The next day, John Newlove talks with Gzowski about poetry. Newlove says there's no reason to write a poem – it's a foolish thing to do. By the way, asks Gzowski, what's this post-modernism anyway? Who knows? they laugh. It doesn't get any better. Is poetry popular? and… John, are you popular? and… are poets making a living at it? Are they like other working people, getting up in the morning, having breakfast, then writing their poems? Name two, challenges John. OK, let's hear you read your poems, and can you talk about what we're supposed to be getting out of it? Are we missing out on something?

The private world of poets writing for themselves and other poets writing for themselves and other poets. But British publishers say poetry is back in style, attributing the surge and flowering of poetic writing and reading to a new aggressive approach to marketing poetry, which has gone a long way toward changing its dry, elitist image.]

From the Rainbucket to the Lawnmower

I'm not surprised
that words are met with silence, even death.
At least today
the pen is mightier than the blade.

For Leonard

How do I love her—
when I got this
you know
mustache headache.

Motions

Be it resolved that
for every undisclosed drop of rain
a leaf like a siren will swirl
on the grave remains of the soldier
who falls in a foreign land

Be it resolved
that for every undisguised shelterless
an appropriate chamber of the house be devoted
as a shrine

Hurry!
with our tophats and lily-white gloves
our hardhats and steel-toed workboots
our friendly sombreros and mystical sunglasses
our debonair scarves and sealskin fashions
hurry down to them

Where is the object of their desire?

a white house in Nova Scotia
or the paleozoic remains of London, Ontario
under the dry autumn leaves in Westmount
or the muzak of an allnight train heading through the northern
                              woods beside the pastel highways
a line drive in the schoolyard of Lawrence, B.C.
or in the room with her in the rue des Ecoles
daisy daisy
or eating penny candy in a concrete cemetery
glued to the throbbing genitals of Money
or awaiting another rush of the tide of the heart
caught up in a streetcorner brawl
or in the center of the center aisle watching the closeup of a gun
the rock roll wine taste grease job in a West Village garage
or sitting in the trees with drums between our knees
behind us, reflected in a pool
or the scarlet silk trousers of the infant Christ
mirrors into mirrors into mirror
or as we forgive those O Canada who trespass against us
sitting between the rows of corn
or back to the perfectly motionless printed letters

the flowers go on opening
or only light just light
yellow heals the right eye
ou un film cheap défrayé
brûler et torcher
ou victoire pas de parfait
dis Manon viens danser le ska
ou le corps—a 150 km/hr sur une route perdue d'Abitibi en
                                    plein été
glazed with rain water
or why are you setting cedar boards daughter around the edge
                                    of your garden
why are you sitting quietly on your shapely legs
folded beneath you on the kitchen counter
or in spring will be crocuses daring the sky to change
sitting alone along the curbs of public buildings

Be it resolved
that youth will pay for the debt they inherited
one catch-22 after another
one addiction after another
one revengeful murder after another
one unwed mother after another
one howling piss party moonlight drunk on the beach
after another
one suicide after another
one runaway prostitute after another
one confused child after another
watching the musical chairs of relationships vanish

Be it resolved
that the malaise is a political cancer
and no amount of poetry will shake its walls
and break its power
for an age of conservatism is upon us
and strips us of our usefulness and dignity
in the face of nuclear supervision

Be it resolved
that our eyes can't resist fire
and our ears are not deaf to the drums of war
that we cannot walk the tightrope of mortality
and not succumb to the memory of our species
under a windblown tree in the clearing

Flamenco

My heart screams with pain
(the night is warm under the stars)
your smell pervades my world, I'm yours.

Do with me on a white charger
until my breath is taken away,
and I lie.

Hold me, never let go;
reincarnate me as you, that I may find myself
in tears, in a crowd, on the metro.

Let us find ourselves
A secret place
In one long drawn-out moan,
make me say, "Uncle!" — I confess
my life has been a sink
of tears and sperm and blood,
and all human joy was sand-heavy on my heart,
afloat on love.

Betrayed by friends, surprised
in any number of familiar places,
I am surprised and want to be surprised only
by you.

Black and white flowers on handkerchiefs.

Hopscotch

            Jump

through   hoops

            for

            love

money   power

            until

            death.

Percussion

begin by

telling the truth about the b
irth of the b
abe

until the heavens crack or
someone cries b
ingo

Around the Point

We pushed off from Tofino in the early morning;
the skies were cloudy.
The gentlest rain recalled the last few days,
but also closed a curtain behind us.
Innocent strokes propelled the kayaks that first day,
advancing to the first beach almost magically,
faster than our thoughts.

The rituals took over:
packing, stuffing, strapping, unstrapping,
unstuffing, unpacking, assembling our eco-tents,
converging on the food.

The food! The food of gods!
whose emissaries, Natasha, Robson,
thought of everything delicious: oysters, brie, feast of salad, pita,
creamy peanut butter and jam, punctuated with that nectar
whose delicious aroma haunts us still—the coffee.

With that coffee we could fly
across the highest swell,
out muscle any tidal pull,
pull the crafts up sandy beaches, past the logs, into the trees.

With that coffee we could brave the freezing creeks,
bathe in icy pools,
splashing and laughing like children.

With that coffee…
never mind, let some of the mystery remain untold,
let future generations learn our secrets
through the whispers of the full white moon.

We soon lost touch with the uncivilized world of work and news;
only Robson, our guru guide,
tuned into warnings on a hidden marine radio.

Robson—unrelenting tireless chief, whose face
grown gaunt from years of battling the elements,
from the harsh climes of Canmore
to the jungles of Bolivia—
greeted us each morning with an ironic smile
which said, "we're moving out".

Once, when with our last remaining ounce of strength
we reached out over the waves for reassurance,
he turned and uttered the magical phrase
"just around the next point".
Of course, around the next point
was just that—the next point, the next *point*.
Who were we to argue?

Wayne, a New York native, each day in court, in a uniform?
A happy face at happy hour? He would paint (he swore)
each jumping salmon, dolphin or whale, whether he saw it or not!

The Kertesz sisters? Pregnant Susan,
who never complained, just leaned over and recycled,
or her sister Martha, peeking through her 12 cameras,
setting her time lapses and, in a halo of flashes,
discovering bliss.

Or Allan and Joan, who flew from Toronto
just to defend our legal right of passage? Allan,
like a frisky teenager, hopping along the beach at dawn,
to bring his Joan her breakfast in bed.

Or the newlyweds Lewis and Jennifer? who appeared to us once
or twice, in a dream,
reporting on remote spots we should see, there–
just around the point. Unlike the rest,
they ignored the official list and brought instead,
chilled wine and rum.

Or the Karen-Karens? and Christine, their leader,
driving away from the buzz of California,
taking turns with Robson, our guide.

Or the other trusty guide, Natasha, whose name
belied her physical strength, who single-handed
carried water tanks, kayak and the *gorp* —
and still managed to smile.

Or Marlene and Tom? who raced to be last
on the beach, last
in the water, first
to the coffee, first to the joke.

Each day the sun beats down more hot than before,
the moon glows brighter in the clear, clean sky;
our sense of beauty is challenged by this god
of nature and holiday
persistently and with good cause.

See where light and colours shine! on sea, on hazy mountain—
how can my imagination not be puffed there,
white capped waves announcing its heartbeat,
white wings of eagles spreading, breaking sky,
white bands of gulls cry loud in joy of a watery feast—
and just as time threatens to finally loosen its claws,
to set me free forever, I see
the white Nimbus waving in greeting, I long to understand
its gesture as welcome, come, and.. become,
when I hear the striking of wood against sand, and it's sad.

August 4, 1993

Lost and Found

Boy meets dog. Boy loses dog.
Boy finds god. Boy loses faith.
Boy finds job. Boy loses job.
Boy meets girl. Boy loses girl.
Boy finds freedom. Boy loses innocence.
Boy finds man. Man loses boy.
Man finds love. Man loses self.
Man finds home. Man loses song.
Man finds children. Man loses wife.
Man finds gold. Man loses gold.
Man finds time. Man loses hair.
Man finds dream. Man loses dream.
Man finds laughter. Man loses time.
Man finds meaning to life. Man loses life.

Into This Space

    light at first penetrates uneasily in long pencil-thin strokes, unsettling dust before moving on, ever upward, bouncing from glass to metal in Pan-like strides yet without any semblance of mischief or grace. Its touch is warm, it's true, yet it pretends not comfort or joy. Impossible to deduce a will moving invisible yet causing enlightenment. Against all odds, the creator walks into the path of light streaming through the crusted window and interrupts the silence with a song. The beams know it not, nor the nocturnal roaches, and the mirror is blind, the dust unforgiving.

Into this space
    water drips mysteriously, avoiding the snare of a tin can with its random bursts. The roof was coated in all the likely places, yet the uneven tap of water persists, a benefit for an unknown tree in an impenetrable forest.

Into this space
    two lovers have escaped to spend an uninterrupted night together. The calm of the neighbourhood does not diminish their fear of discovery. They nearly trip upon a cot, over which he spreads his long black coat, then sits to remove his boots. She is cold under the cover, sitting and hugging her knees, and rocking, attempting to see through the dark. His whispers grow more urgent, yet she moves not, and is silent. He laughs into the silence, to which she replies with a whisper, then a kiss, and a touch.

Into this space
    a group of squatters have begun moving furniture, a cooking range, portable heaters, boxes of clothing, canned pasta foods. Three men struggle with a washtub through the hallway. As one iron leg catches on a loose floorboard, they're forced to retreat and examine the remaining distance. Children scream and run up the stairs, followed by a small but loud scruffy white dog. The women hang sheets to divide the sleeping quarters. Two old men sit at a table, tapping black and red pieces on a checkerboard, arguing, punctuating their curses with spitting on the floor.

Into this space
    Fellini and then Ferlinghetti lured a plump girl of nineteen who has lured three young boys who carry bottles of wine and baguettes. The youngest drags the others' schoolbooks behind him, tied together with a simple belt. How she dances and twirls, drinks and gesticulates with the bread, now like a proud soldier with his gun, now a focused batter with his powerful bat. How the boys cheer and stamp their feet. Popping a cork, she lifts the bottle high, lifts her skirts, and smashes an empty against the brick wall. The youngest begins to cry at that, while the other two hold him back from running out. Loud whispers in his ear do still him, and he raises a new bottle high and thrusts it out to her.

Into this space
    a burly seascape painter drops his easel near a wide window. Sneezing twice, he struggles with the latch, and succeeds to open the window but not without a big bang which threatens to smash the frail panes. Examining the room from different angles, he retreats, reappearing with two black suitcases, which he drags beside the easel, emptying the contents into one pile. A large blue cloth is last to emerge, which he spreads out on the floor with great care. Now naked, he lies on his back, hands clasped on his chest, eyes open, staring at the ceiling.

Into this space
    a general will order his men to fire. Positions had been taken only hours before, no warning will be given, no inquiry made as to the occupants' identities or choices (whether, indeed there were occupants, and, if so, were they the cause of the maneuver). The instructions were simple, continue firing until the building is brought down to the ground. The general is not one to question his orders; he has read the handwritten note many times over. There is no reason given, only an address, underlined with three heavy strokes of the pen, a brief statement of purpose, and an indecipherable signature the general took for the Secretary of the Interior. He was not going to take any chances either; a tank was rolled within thirty feet, two truckloads of recent recruits were dispersed in small groups to circle the building. First, the lines of communication to the building are severed. Next, traffic is rerouted, and, as the last voices of soldiers become less audible, there remains only the wait until the word is given.

Into this space
     the word is given by the poet with the mustache headache, fighting off impossible demands on his flesh, and his bloodtype. To be known for one who "caught a glimpse of the eternal, despite clearly posted signs to the contrary" he launches one final desperate metaphor and disappears.

Into this space
     you enter alone, bearing your heart, mind and body. The poem is illuminated upon the wall of your mind, it reminds you of dream in which you were afraid and you knelt before your saviour and said I am so afraid please help and the reply was laughter and shame, you shielded your eyes with your hands and they were wet and they were bloody and you screamed and awoke in the bed of a stranger; the poem strips you bare while you're listening, the poem enters your body as an orgasm.

Into this space
     seven poets retreat in the heat of writing. In time, they find the perfect combination of form and image — the father hitching white clouds to white horses. Immediately, they are rewarded with the appearance of a great ark, literally floating above the times, a vehicle transformed into a kind of postmodern muse: dispensing favours but coin operated.

Books by Tom Konyves

Poetry

No Parking (1978)
Poetry in Performance (1982)
Ex Perimeter (1988)